INTERESTING FACTS
ABOUT NAPOLEON
BONAPARTE

BY EDDIE ALFARO

NAPOLÉON BONAPARTE WAS EMPEROR OF THE FRENCH AS NAPOLÉON I FROM 1804 UNTIL 1814.

HIS PARENTS AND CLOSE ACQUAINTANCES CALLED HIM BY HIS NICKNAME, NABULIO.

NAPOLEON DISCOVERED THE ROSETTA STONE, IT PLAYED A VITAL PART IN DECIPHERING EGYPTIAN HIEROGLYPHS.

NAPOLEON COULD THINK AND SPEAK SO FAST THAT HE WAS ABLE TO DICTATE FIVE LETTERS TO HIS SECRETARIES AT THE SAME TIME.

HE HAS BECOME SYNONYMOUS WITH THE TERM "NAPOLEON COMPLEX", USED TO CHARACTERISE SHORT, OVERLY AGGRESSIVE PEOPLE. BUT NAPOLEON WAS 5 FEET 7 WHICH WAS AN AVERAGE HEIGHT FOR THE TIME.

NAPOLEON WROTE A ROMANCE NOVEL, "CLISSON ET EUGENIE".

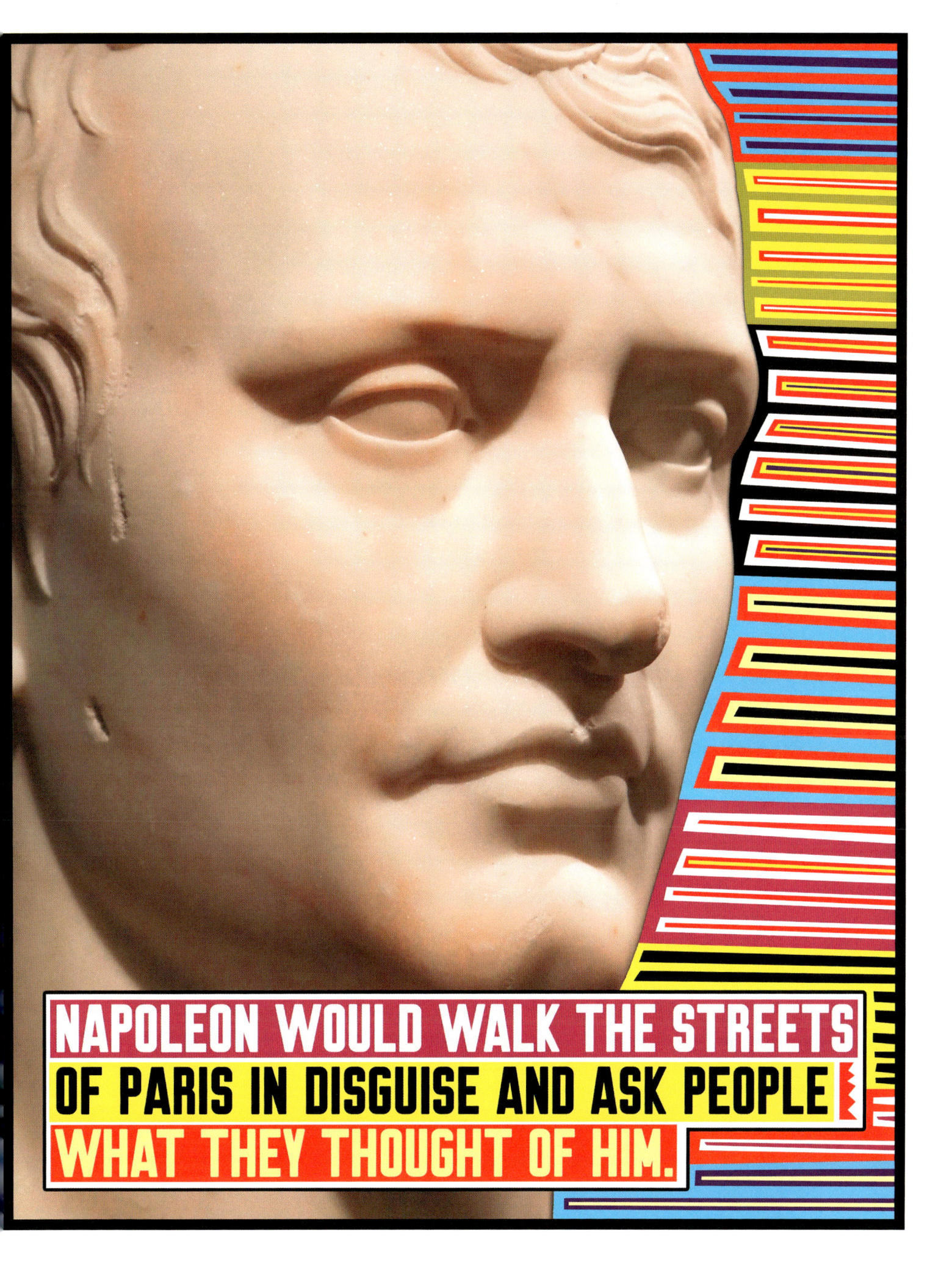

NAPOLEON WOULD WALK THE STREETS OF PARIS IN DISGUISE AND ASK PEOPLE WHAT THEY THOUGHT OF HIM.

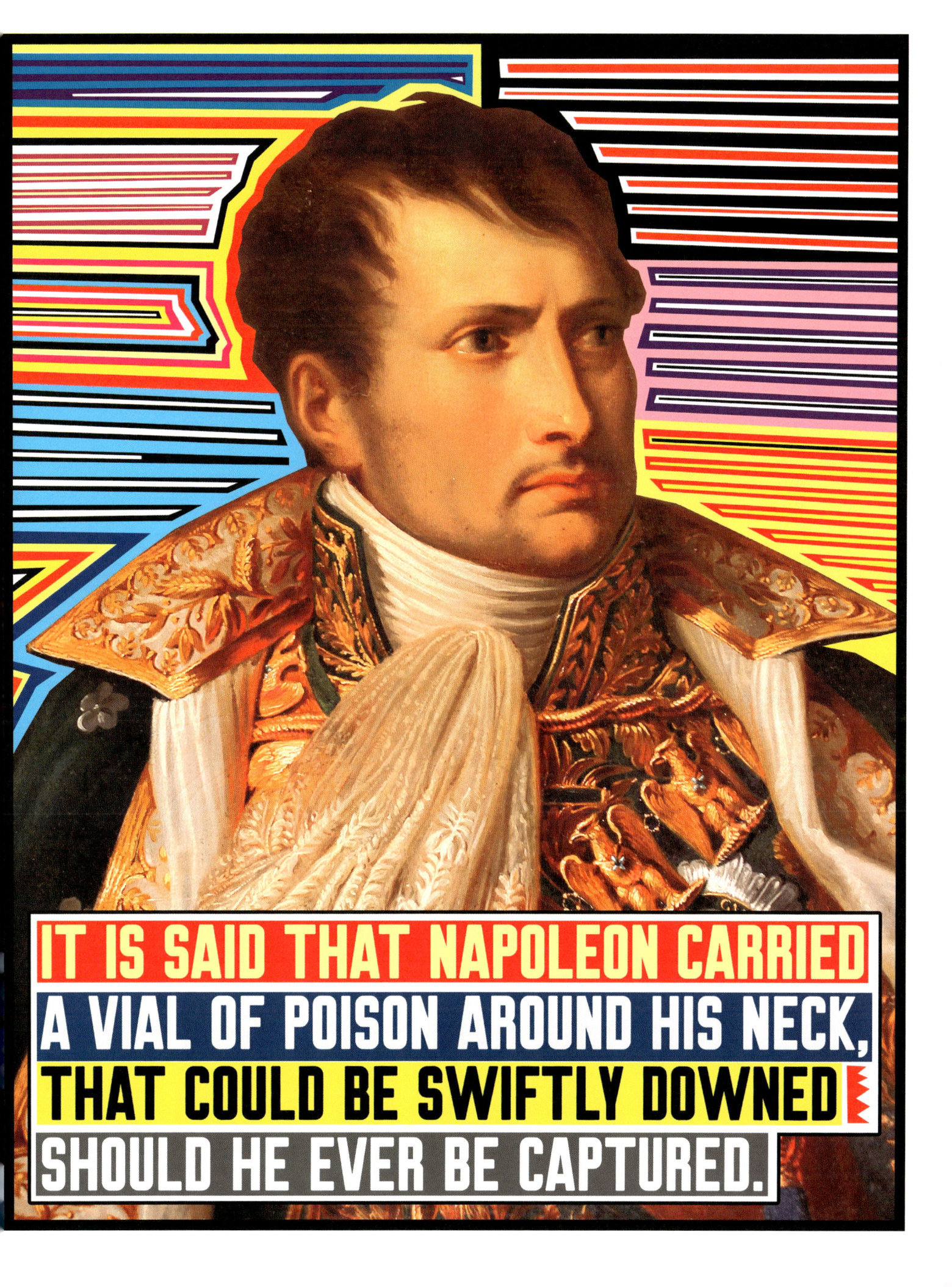

IT IS SAID THAT NAPOLEON CARRIED A VIAL OF POISON AROUND HIS NECK, THAT COULD BE SWIFTLY DOWNED SHOULD HE EVER BE CAPTURED.

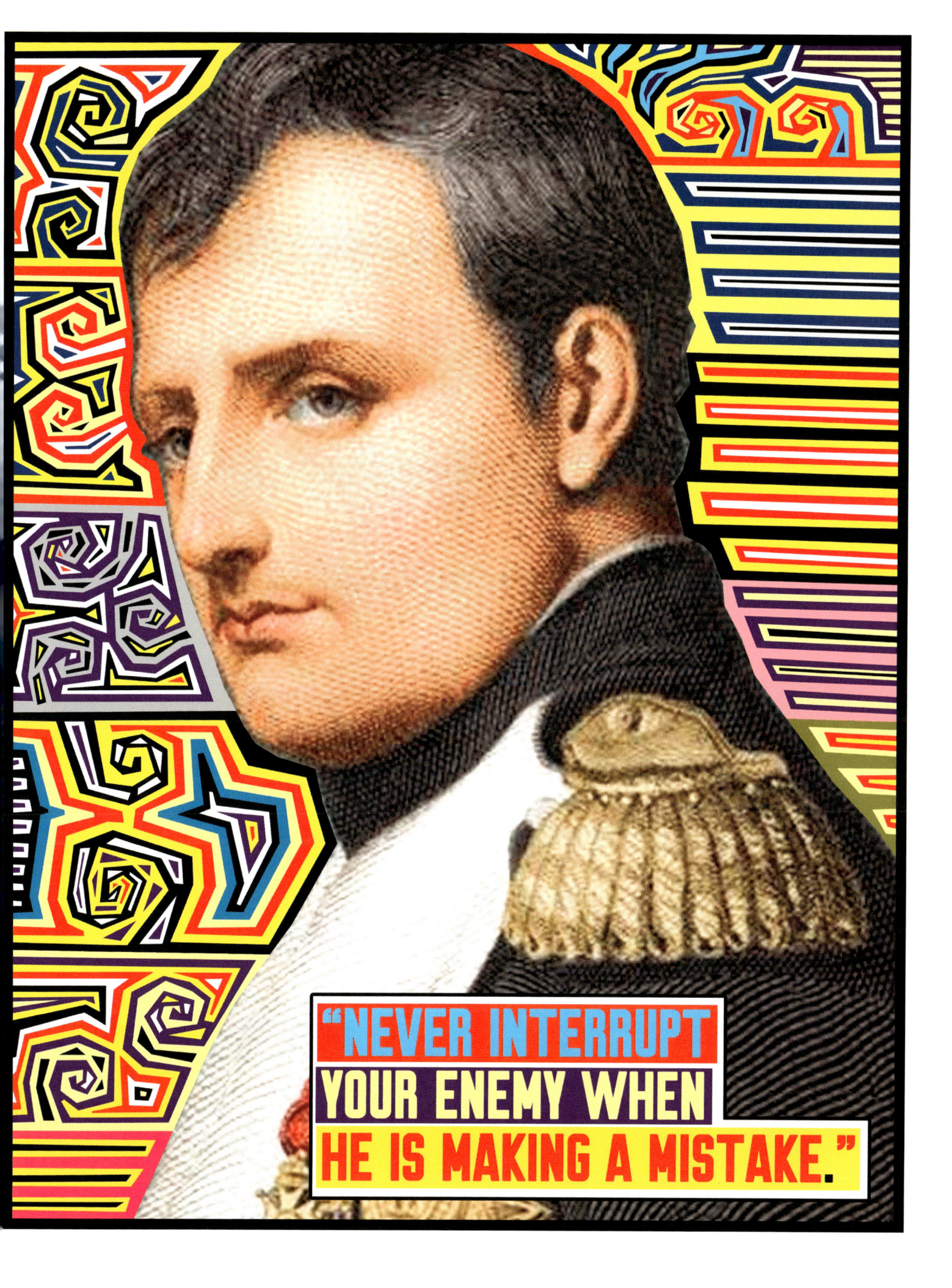

"NEVER INTERRUPT YOUR ENEMY WHEN HE IS MAKING A MISTAKE."

WHILE IN EXILE, NAPOLEON PUBLISHED HIS MEMOIRS AND WROTE A BOOK ABOUT THE LIFE OF JULIUS CAESAR.

BRAILLE WRITING WAS CREATED FROM A SYSTEM OF COMMUNICATION NAPOLEON CREATED FOR HIS SOLDIERS.

PEOPLE DRIVE ON THE RIGHT SIDE OF THE ROAD BECAUSE OF NAPOLEON. HE ENFORCED IT FOR HORSEBACK TRAFFIC THROUGHOUT HIS TERRITORIES. HE DID NOT CONQUER BRITAIN SO LEFT HAND DRIVING REMAINS THERE.

BEETHOVEN'S 3RD SYMPHONY WAS ORIGINALLY NAMED "BONAPARTE" AND WAS DEDICATED TO NAPOLEON, THEN A FRENCH GENERAL.

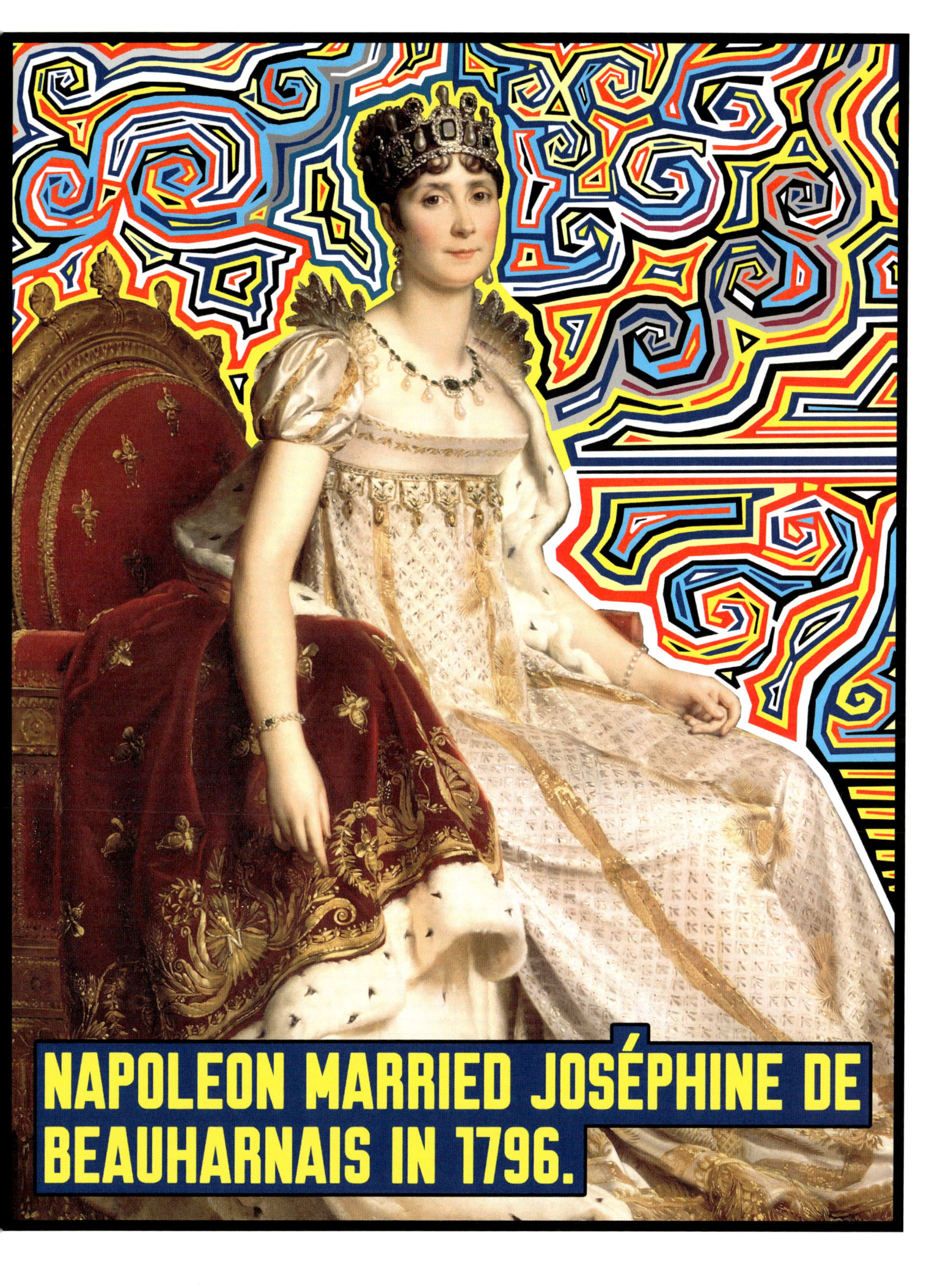

NAPOLEON MARRIED JOSÉPHINE DE BEAUHARNAIS IN 1796.

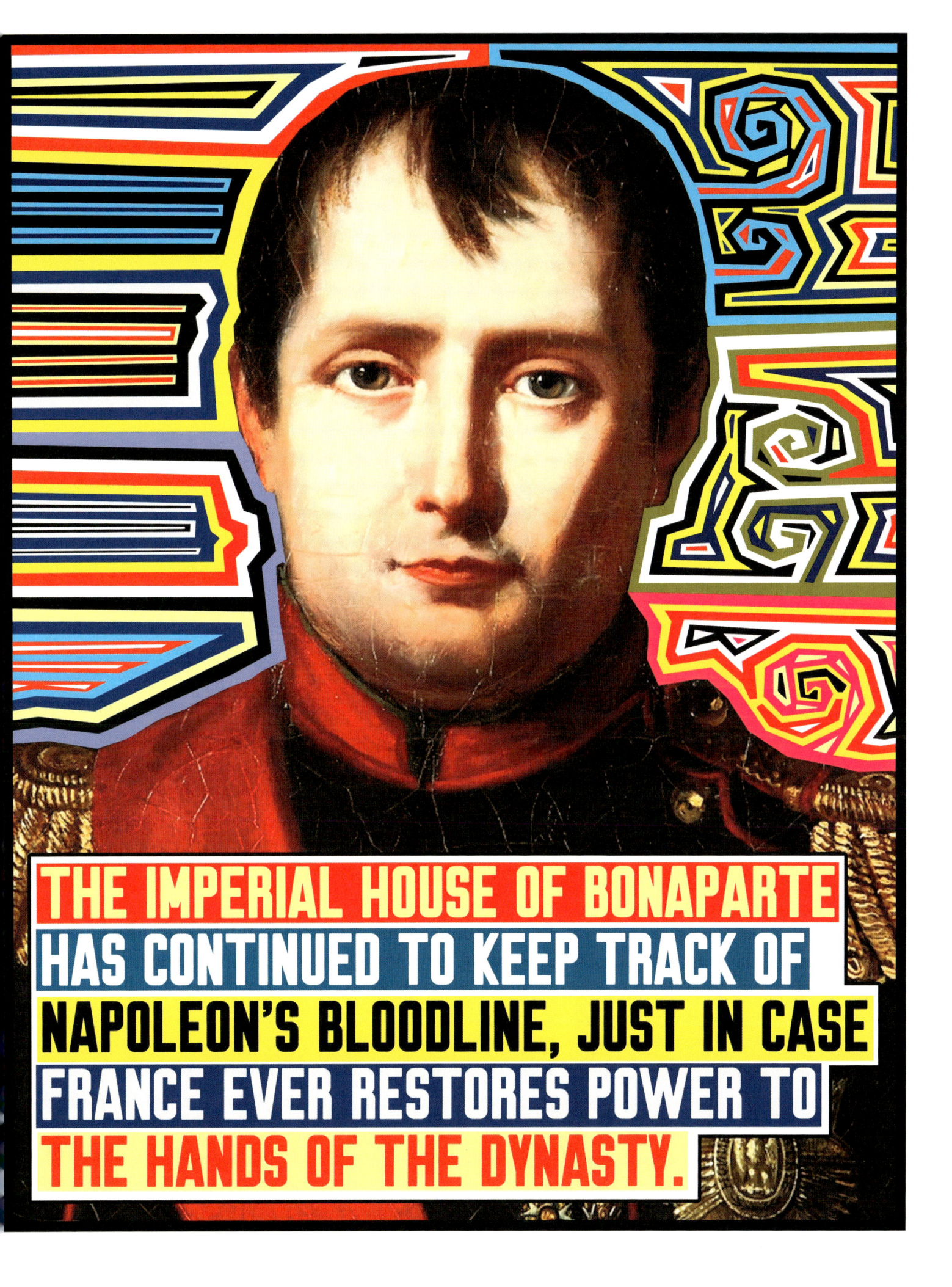

THE IMPERIAL HOUSE OF BONAPARTE HAS CONTINUED TO KEEP TRACK OF NAPOLEON'S BLOODLINE, JUST IN CASE FRANCE EVER RESTORES POWER TO THE HANDS OF THE DYNASTY.

WHILE NAPOLEON WAS IN POWER, THE MONA LISA WAS HUNG IN HIS BEDROOM.

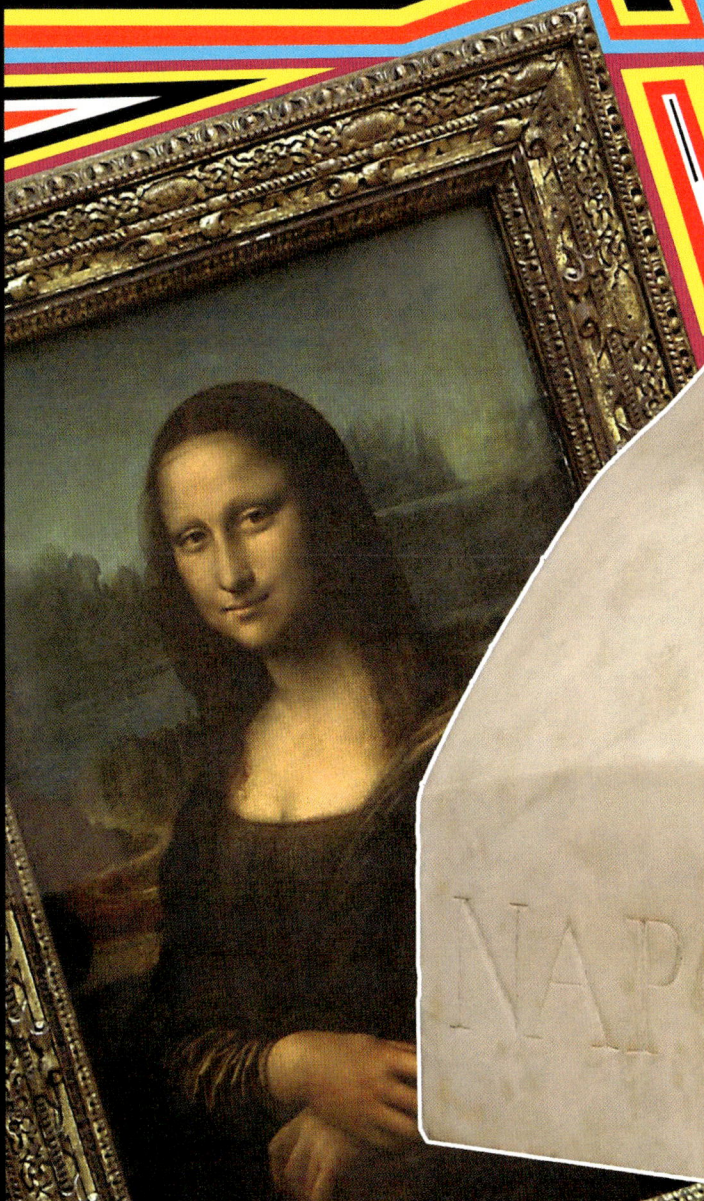

DURING HIS MILITARY CAMPAIGN TO SEIZE EGYPT, NAPOLEON BROUGHT ALONG 150 SCIENTISTS, ENGINEERS, AND SCHOLARS TO SURVEY THE TOPOGRAPHY, ENVIRONMENT, CULTURE, AND HISTORY OF EGYPT.

THE AMERICAN REVOLUTION WOULD NOT HAVE BEEN POSSIBLE WITHOUT SUPPORT FROM FRANCE, WHO SENT MONEY AND ARMS TO AMERICAN REVOLUTIONARIES.

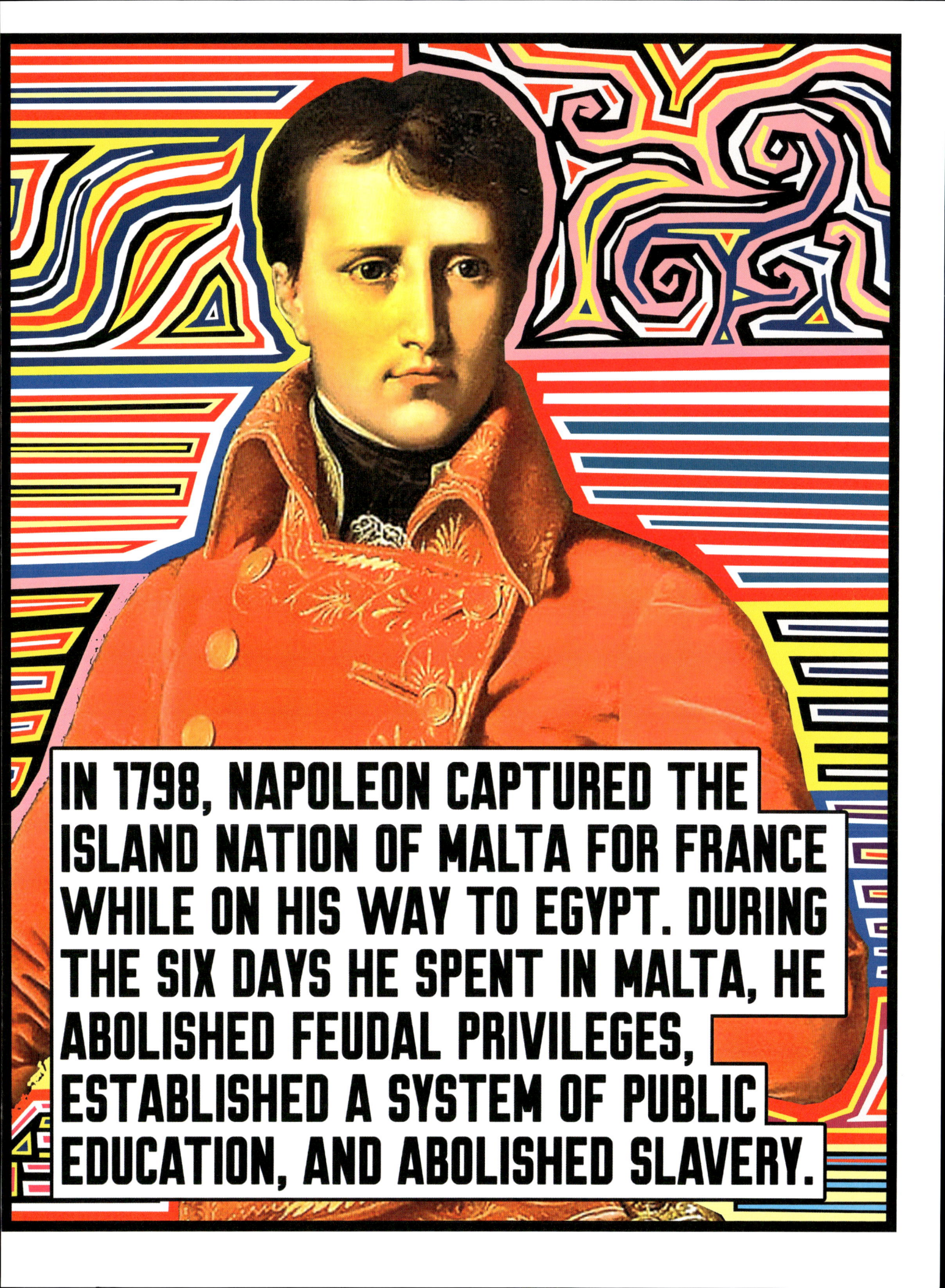

IN 1798, NAPOLEON CAPTURED THE ISLAND NATION OF MALTA FOR FRANCE WHILE ON HIS WAY TO EGYPT. DURING THE SIX DAYS HE SPENT IN MALTA, HE ABOLISHED FEUDAL PRIVILEGES, ESTABLISHED A SYSTEM OF PUBLIC EDUCATION, AND ABOLISHED SLAVERY.

BONAPARTE LAID THE FOUNDATION FOR MODERN FRENCH EDUCATION AND CREATED A SET OF LAWS KNOWN AS THE NAPOLEONIC CODE, BASED ON COMMON SENSE AND EQUALITY.

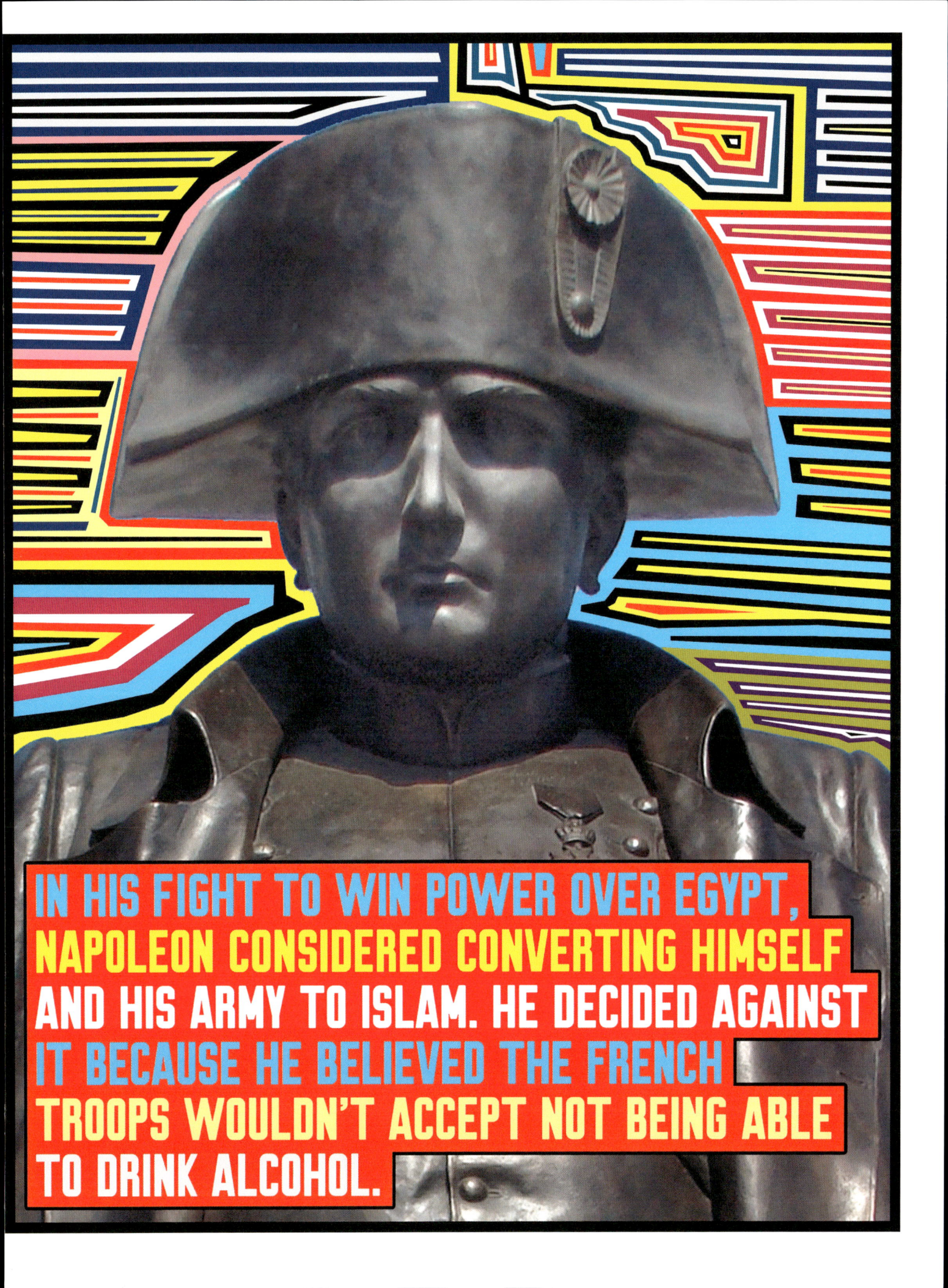

IN HIS FIGHT TO WIN POWER OVER EGYPT, NAPOLEON CONSIDERED CONVERTING HIMSELF AND HIS ARMY TO ISLAM. HE DECIDED AGAINST IT BECAUSE HE BELIEVED THE FRENCH TROOPS WOULDN'T ACCEPT NOT BEING ABLE TO DRINK ALCOHOL.

OFTEN CREDITED WITH THE PHRASE "A PICTURE IS WORTH 1,000 WORDS," WHAT NAPOLEON ACTUALLY SAID WAS: "A GOOD SKETCH IS BETTER THAN A LONG SPEECH."

SOME BELIEVE THAT NAPOLEON HAD A PHOTOGRAPHIC MEMORY AND COULD INSTANTLY RECALL VAST AMOUNTS OF INFORMATION.

NAPOLEON JAILED 13 CATHOLIC CARDINALS FOR NOT ATTENDING HIS SECOND MARRIAGE. HIS OFFICERS KIDNAPPED POPE PIUS VII AND HELD HIM CAPTIVE FOR FIVE YEARS.

BONAPARTE.

"IMAGINATION RULES THE WORLD."

A BRIEF HISTORY OF NAPOLEON BONAPARTE:

NAPOLEON BONAPARTE WAS BORN IN AJACCIO, CORSICA, ON THE AUGUST 15, 1769.

HIS FATHER WAS CARLO BUONAPARTE, AN IMPORTANT ATTORNEY WHO REPRESENTED CORSICA AT THE COURT OF THE FRENCH KING.

NAPOLEON HAD FOUR BROTHERS AND THREE SISTERS.

HE WAS ABLE TO ATTEND SCHOOL AND GET A GOOD EDUCATION.

NAPOLEON GRADUATED FROM THE ECOLE MILITAIRE IN PARIS, AND BECAME A GENERAL AT THE YOUNG AGE OF 26.

WHILE NAPOLEON WAS IN CORSICA, THE FRENCH REVOLUTION OCCURRED IN PARIS, FRANCE. THE PEOPLE REVOLTED AGAINST THE KING OF FRANCE AND TOOK CONTROL OF THE COUNTRY.

NAPOLEON'S ALLIED HIMSELF WITH A GROUP OF THE REVOLUTIONARIES CALLED THE JACOBINS. HE BECAME THE ARTILLERY COMMANDER AT THE SIEGE OF TOULON IN 1793.

HIS MILITARY LEADERSHIP IN WAS RECOGNIZED BY THE LEADERS OF FRANCE AND, AT THE AGE OF 24, HE WAS PROMOTED TO THE POSITION OF BRIGADIER GENERAL.

IN 1796, NAPOLEON WAS GIVEN COMMAND OF THE FRENCH ARMY IN ITALY. HE DROVE THE AUSTRIANS OUT OF ITALY AND BECAME A NATIONAL HERO.

THE POLITICAL CLIMATE IN FRANCE WAS CHANGING. TOGETHER WITH HIS ALLIES, INCLUDING HIS BROTHER LUCIEN, NAPOLEON FORMED A NEW GOVERNMENT CALLED THE CONSULATE. NAPOLEON GAVE HIMSELF THE TITLE OF FIRST CONSUL. HIS POWERS ESSENTIALLY MADE HIM DICTATOR OF FRANCE.

AS THE DICTATOR OF FRANCE, NAPOLEON CREATED THE FAMOUS NAPOLEONIC CODE. THIS CODE SAID THAT GOVERNMENT POSITIONS WOULD NOT BE GIVEN BASED ON A PERSON'S BIRTH OR RELIGION, BUT ON THEIR QUALIFICATIONS AND ABILITY.

NAPOLEON'S POWER AND CONTROL GREW WITH HIS REFORMS. IN 1804, HE WAS CROWNED THE FIRST EMPEROR FRANCE.

SOON FRANCE WAS AT WAR WITH BRITAIN, AUSTRIA, AND RUSSIA. HE DEFEATED THE AUSTRIAN AND RUSSIAN ARMIES AT THE BATTLE OF AUSTERLITZ IN 1805. NAPOLEON EXPANDED THE FRENCH EMPIRE. FRANCE CONTROLLED MUCH OF EUROPE FROM SPAIN TO THE BORDERS OF RUSSIA.

IN 1812, NAPOLEON MADE HIS FIRST MAJOR MISTAKE. HE DECIDED TO INVADE RUSSIA. IT WAS A DISASTER. MOST OF HIS ARMY HAD DIED FROM THE WEATHER OR STARVED TO DEATH.

EUROPE NOW TURNED ON NAPOLEON NOW HAD TOO SMALL AN ARMY, WAS FORCED INTO EXILE ON THE ISLAND OF ELBA IN 1814.

NAPOLEON ESCAPED FROM ELBA IN 1815.

THE ARMY BACKED NAPOLEON AFTER HIS ESCAPE AND HE TOOK OVER CONTROL OF PARIS FOR A PERIOD CALLED THE HUNDRED DAYS.

THE REST OF EUROPE GATHERED THEIR ARMIES AND MET HIM AT WATERLOO.

NAPOLEON WAS DEFEATED AT THE BATTLE OF WATERLOO ON JUNE 18, 1815 AND WAS ONCE AGAIN FORCED INTO EXILE. THIS TIME ON THE ISLAND OF SAINT HELENA.

NAPOLEON DIED AFTER SIX YEARS OF EXILE ON SAINT HELENA ON MAY 5, 1821.

THE TOMB OF NAPOLEON.

THANK YOU.

THE END.

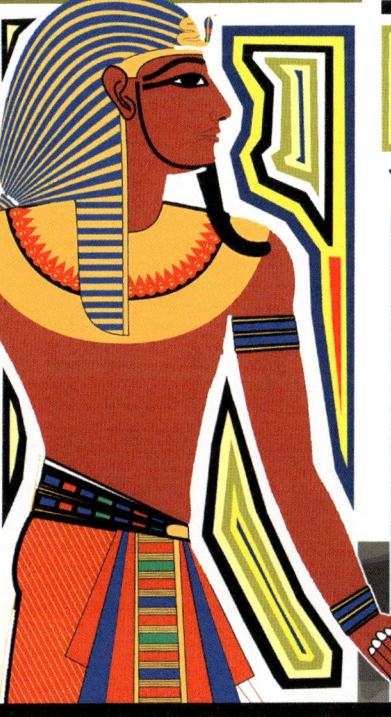
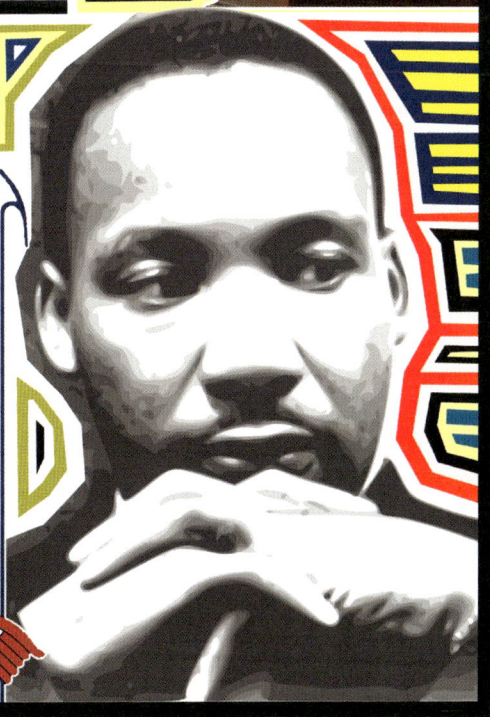

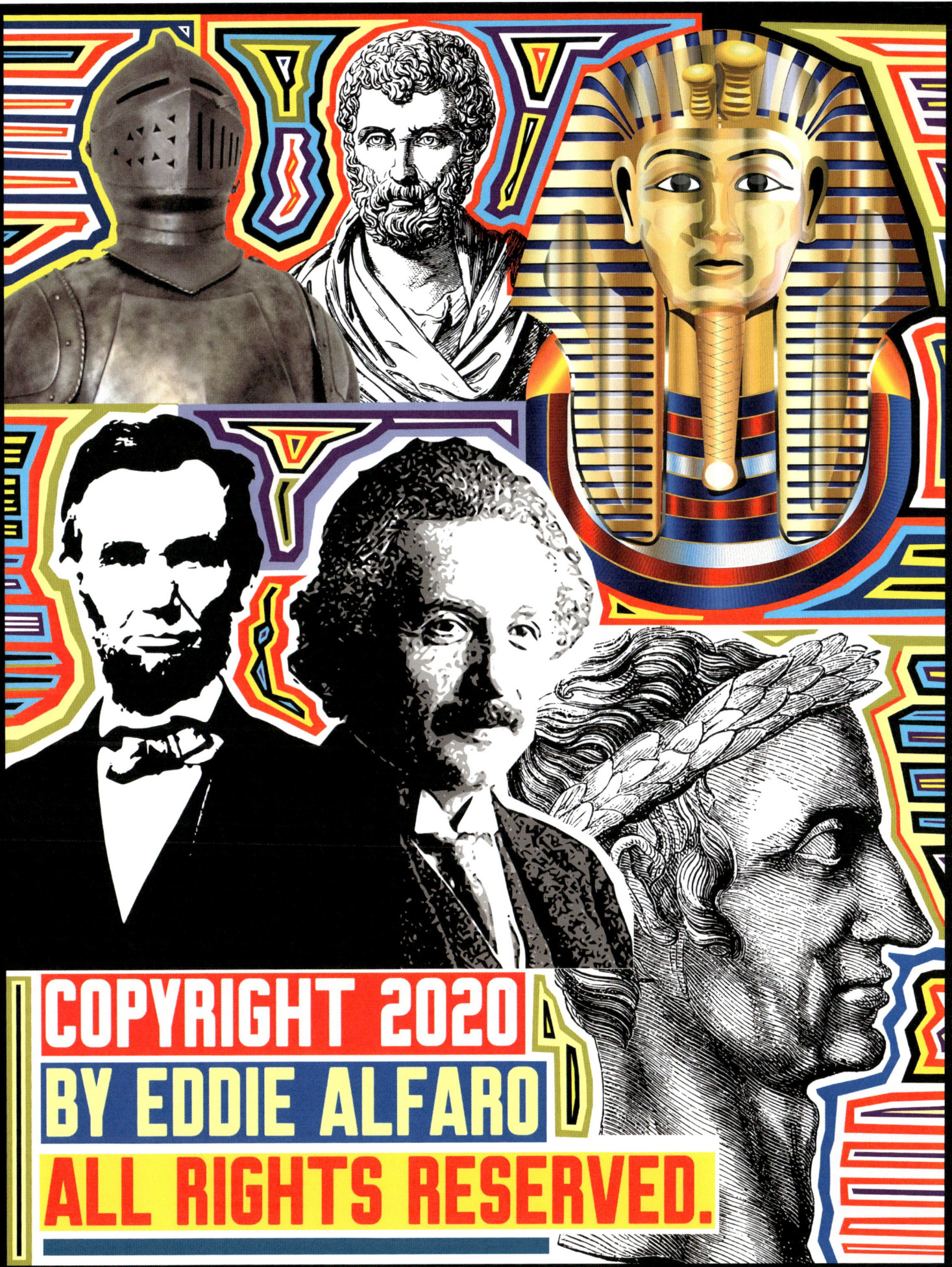

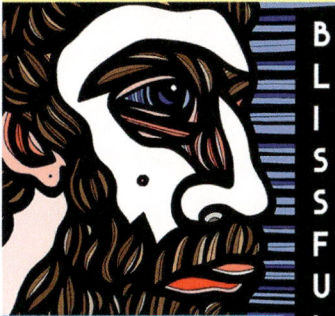

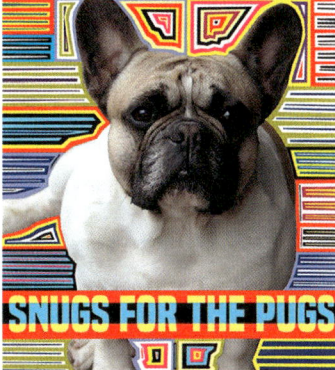

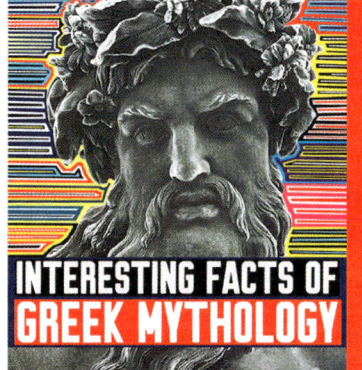

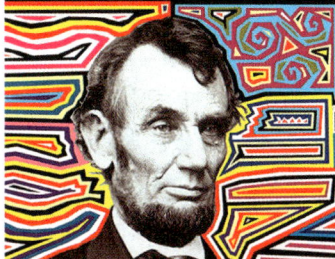

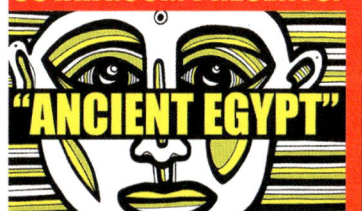

Printed in Great Britain
by Amazon